Santa Barbara Coloring Book

Illustrated by Monique Littlejohn

Please use crayon or pencil when coloring the pages. This paper will not hold up to most permanent markers. Permanent markers will cause bleeding and tearing of the pages.

Coloring Pages List

Santa Barbara Mission exterior

Santa Barbara Mission Interior

Pastels for iMadonarri Street Painting Festival

iMadonarri 2015 Star Trek Bear and others

Our Lady of Sorrows Catholic Church tower

Historic Presidio

Red Tile Roofs

Santa Barbara County Courthouse

Dolphin Fountain

Stearns Wharf

Santa Barbara Shellfish Company

Madame Rosinka on Stearns Wharf

Madame Rosinka window

Surfer walking along Ledbetter Beach

East Beach Volleyball Courts

Elephant Seals

Sea Anemone in a tidepool

Humpback whale breach

Monarch butterfly

Bees on white flower

Santa Barbara Car Show on State St

Open car hoods at Santa Barbara Car Show

Arlington Theatre

Ben Franklin sculpture in La Arcada

La Arcada

Cabrillo Boulevard

Sailboat Race

Summer Solstice float

Cascarones for Fiesta

Traditional Religious Figure in Fiesta Parade

Flamenco Dancer and Mariachis in Fiesta Parade

Equestrian Parade going down State St.

Saint Barbara for Fiesta

Male Mariachi at Fiesta Parade

Amtrak Pacific Surfliner at Santa Barbara Train Station

Flamingo at Santa Barbara Zoo

Gorilla at Santa Barbara Zoo

Macaw at Santa Barbara Zoo

Pierre La Fond wine barrels and cat

Wine barrels and flowers

Farmers Market pumpkins

Santa Barbara Public Library fountain

Lobero Theatre

Granada Theatre

Santa Barbara Museum of Natural History

Cold Spring Bridge

UCSB Tower

Lotuses at Lotusland

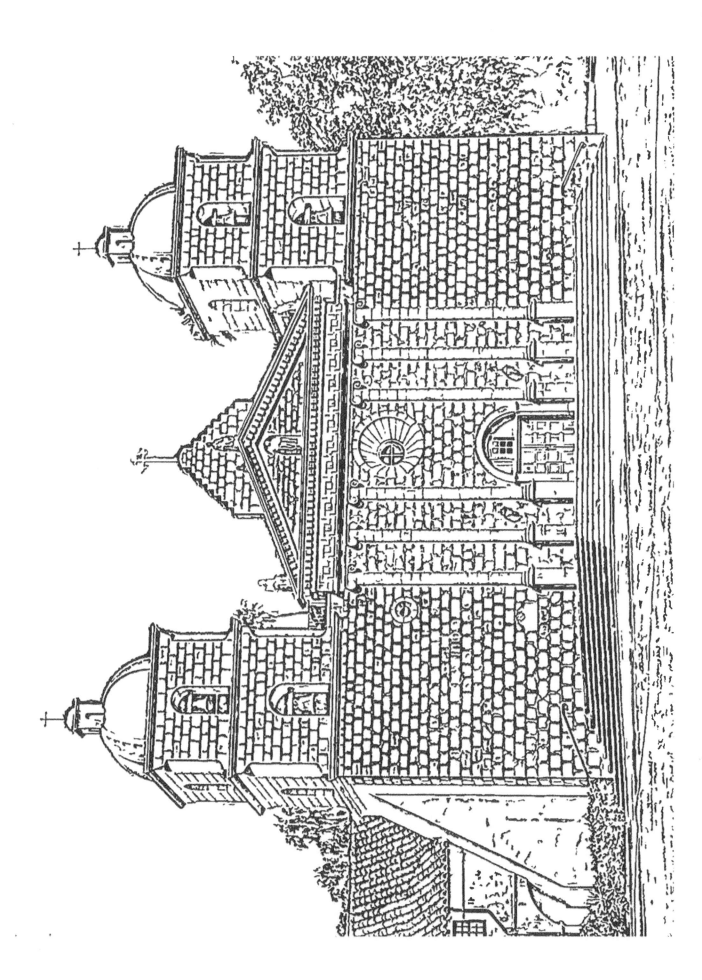

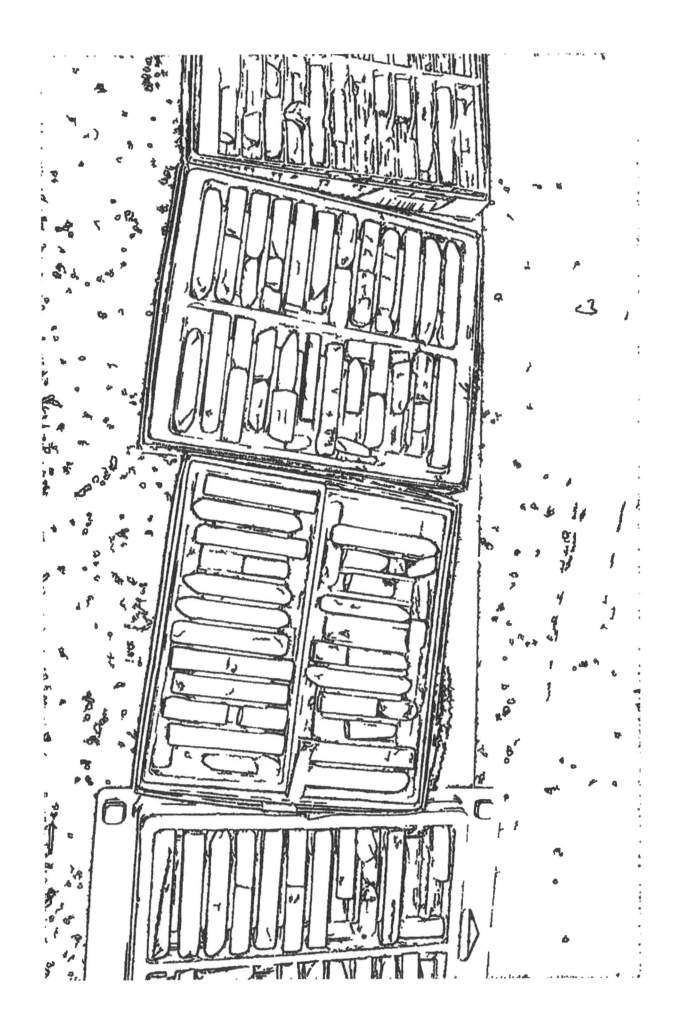

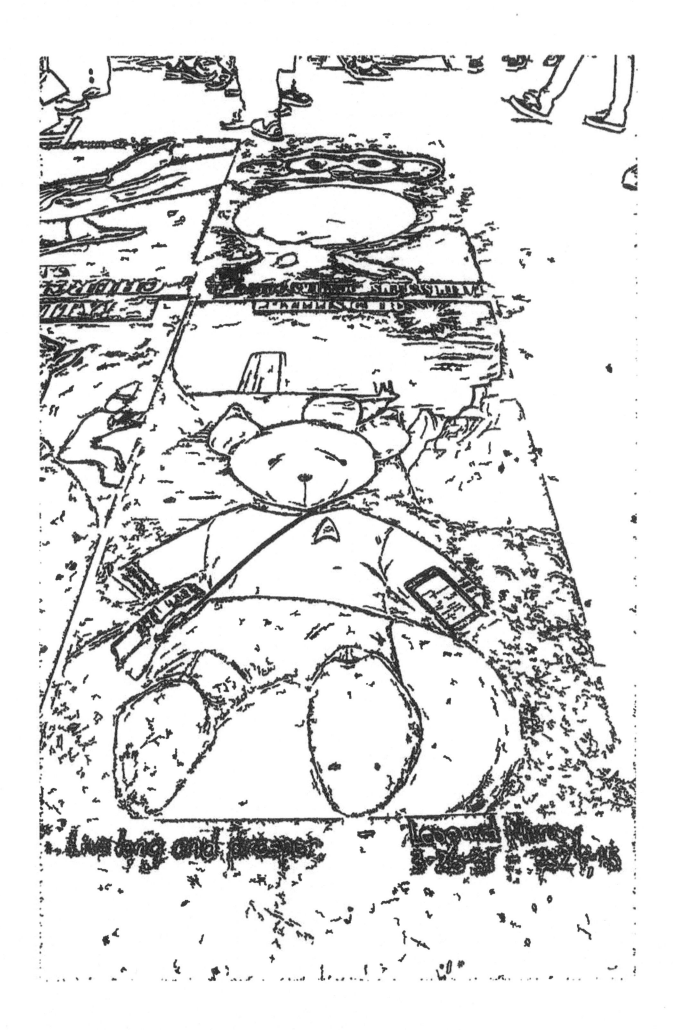

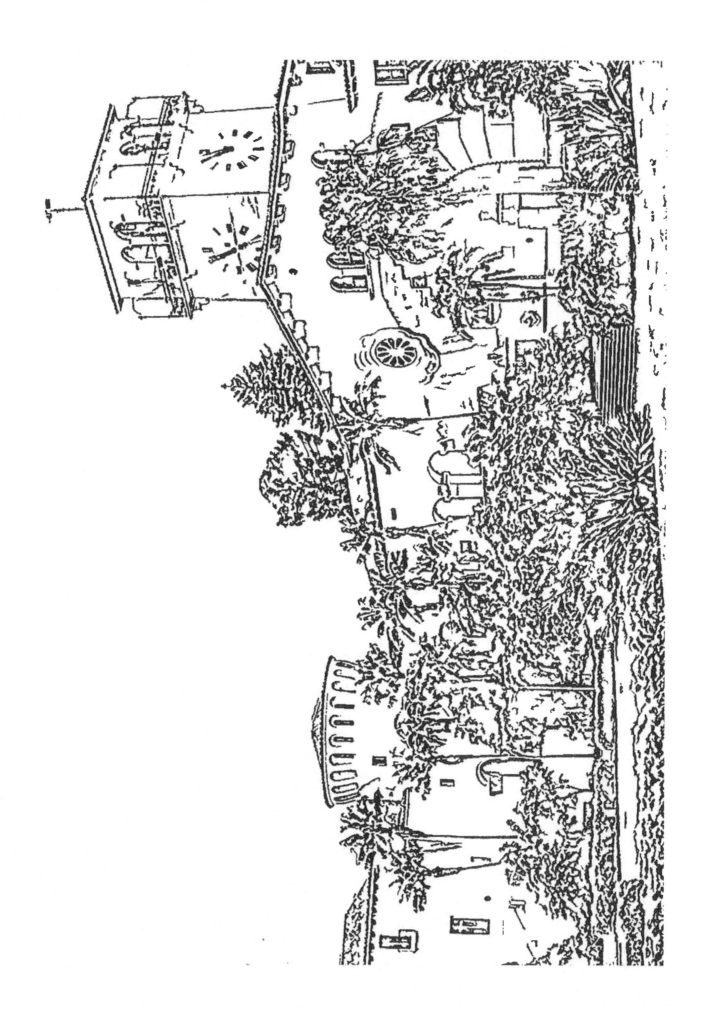

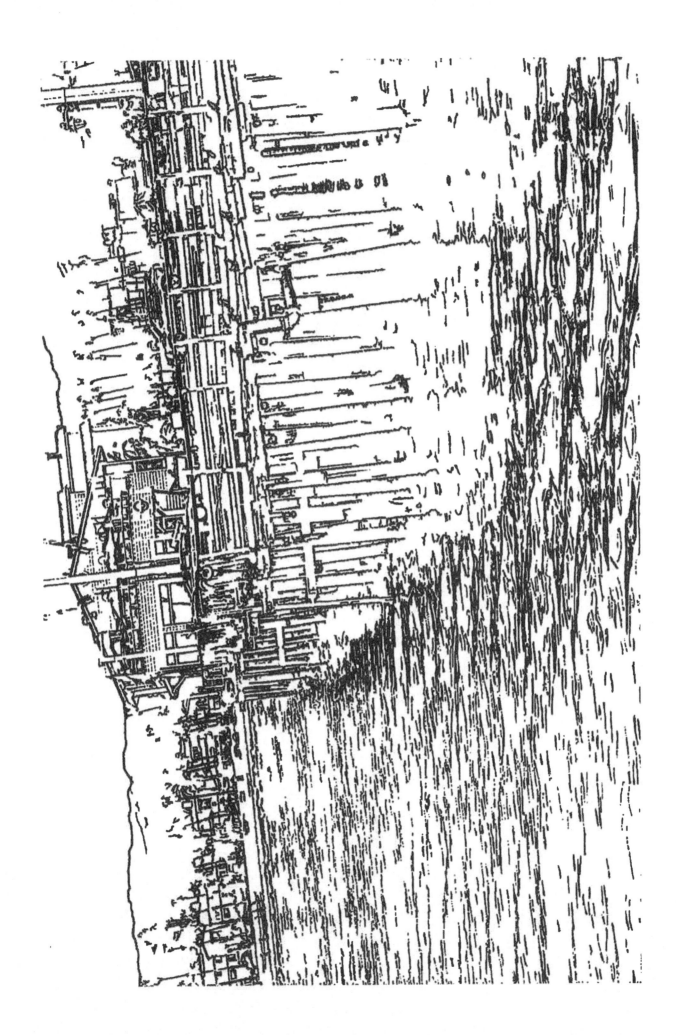

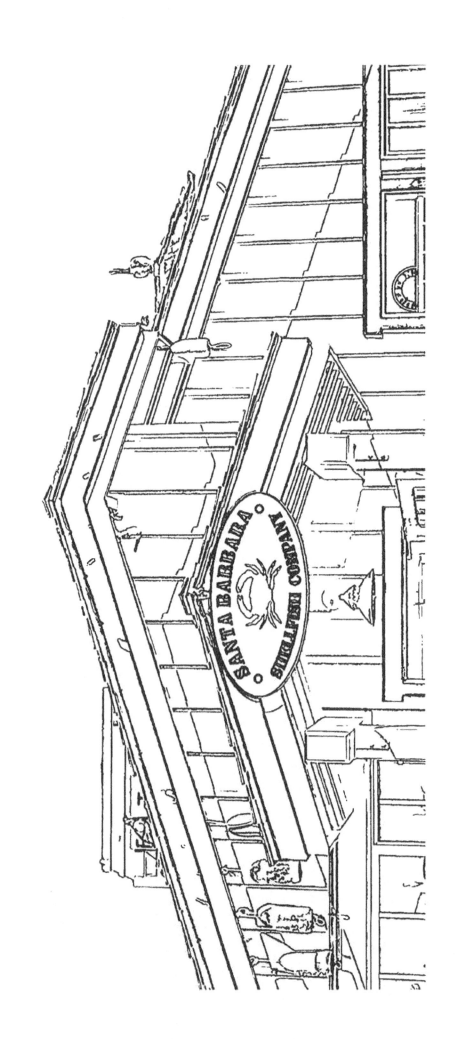

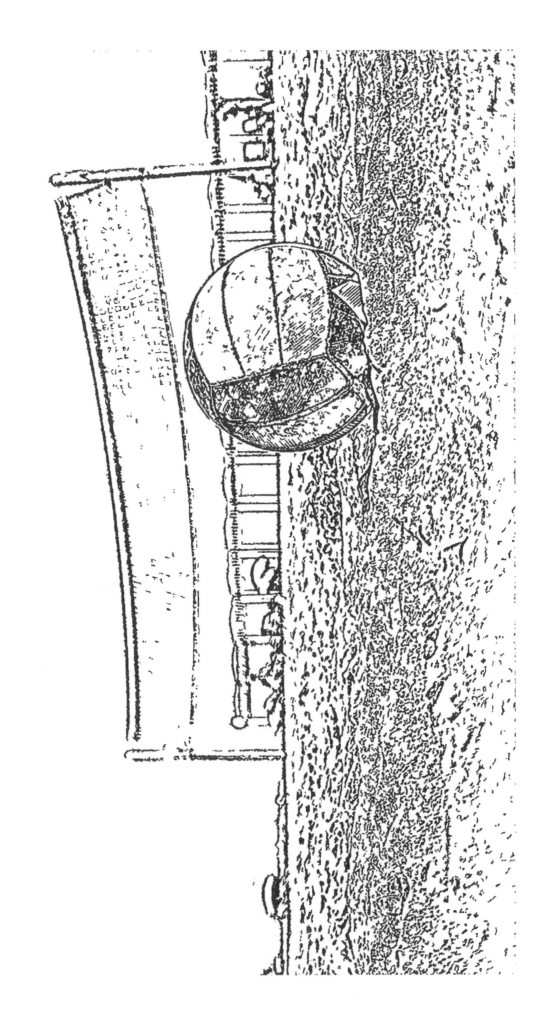

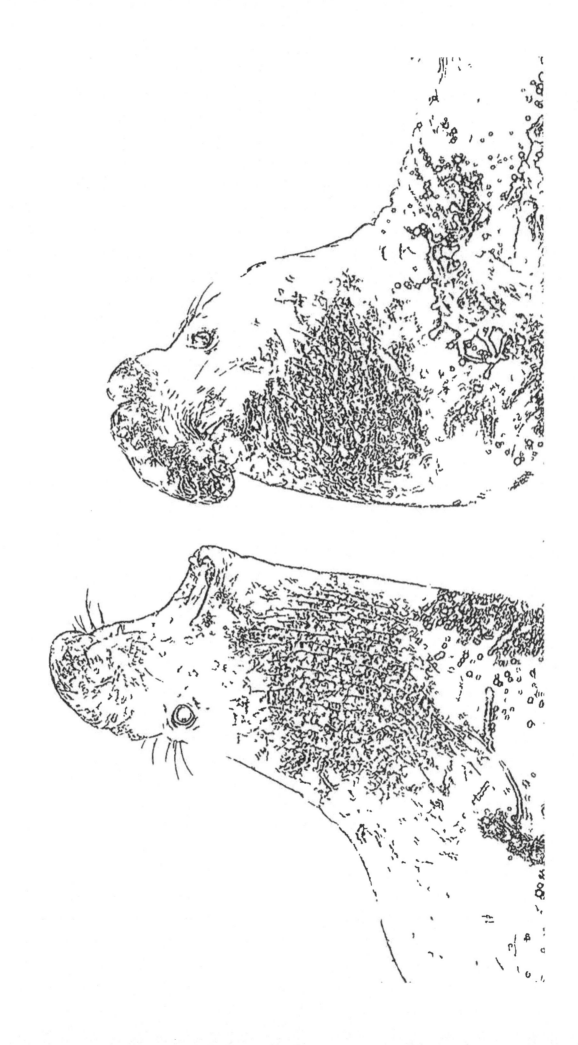

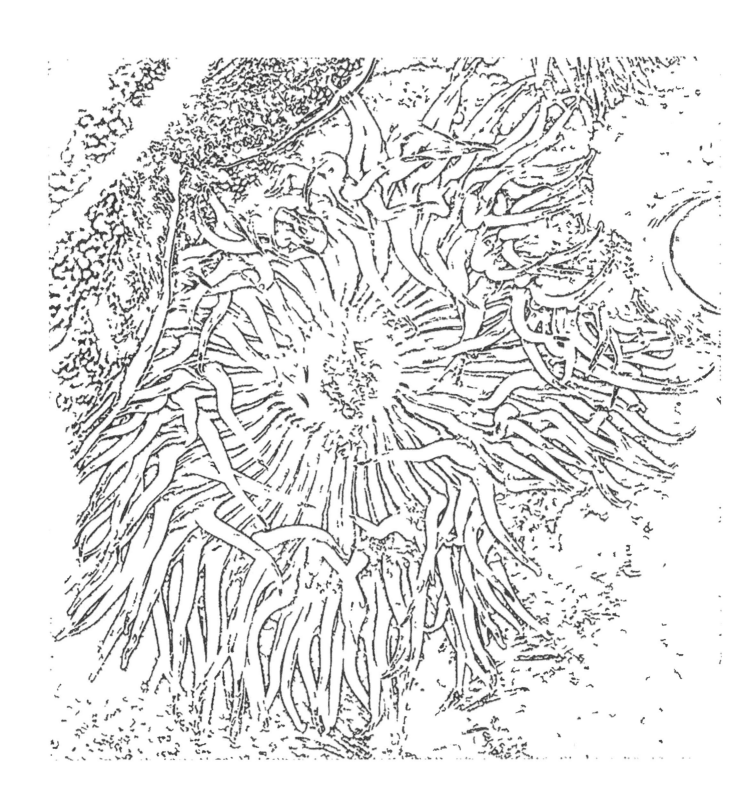

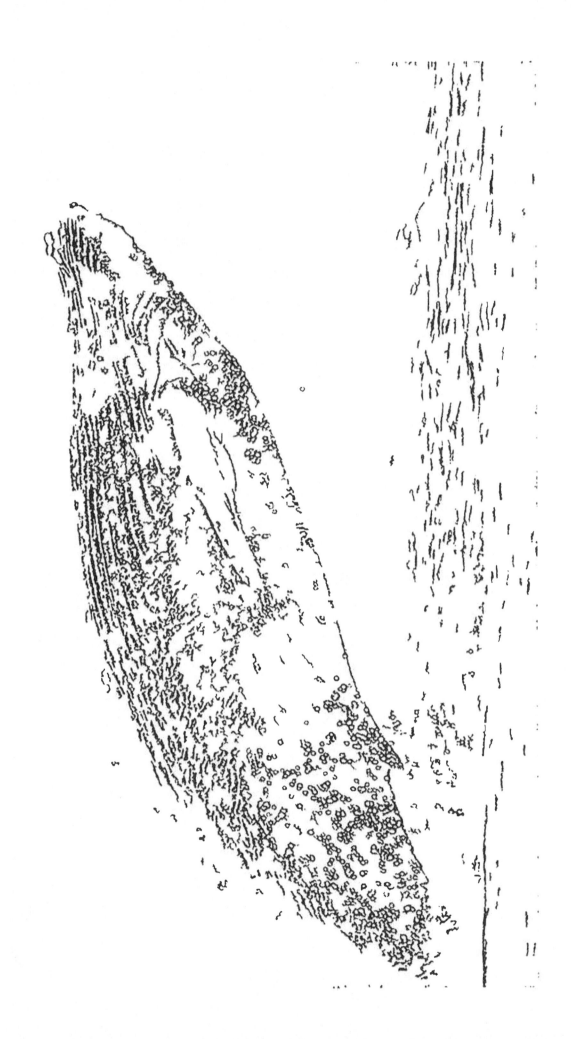

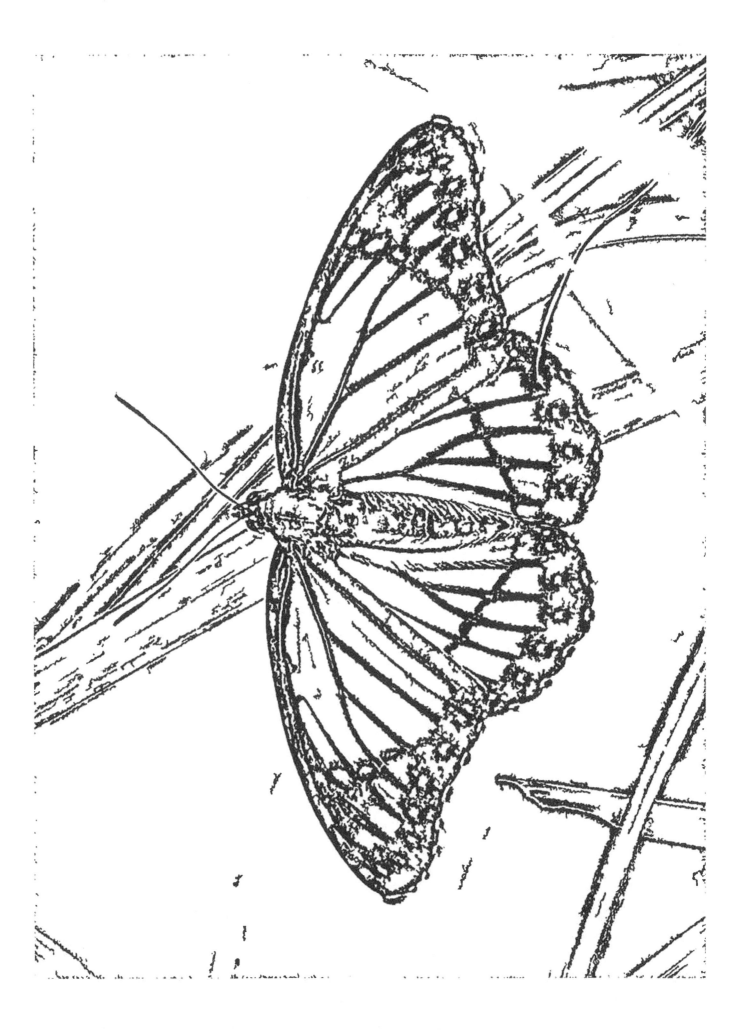

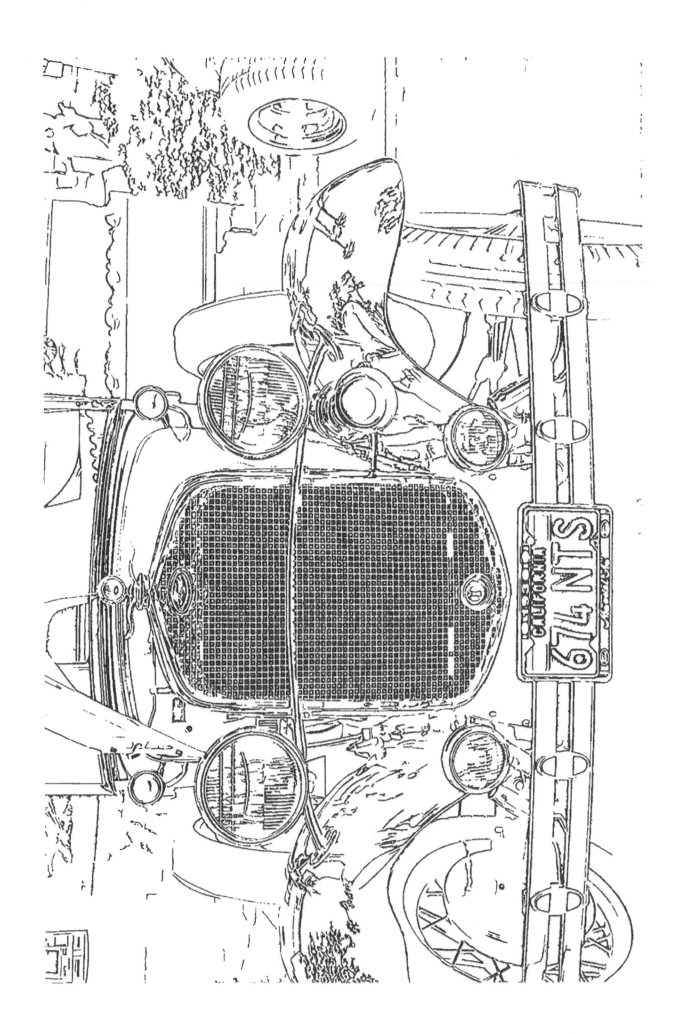

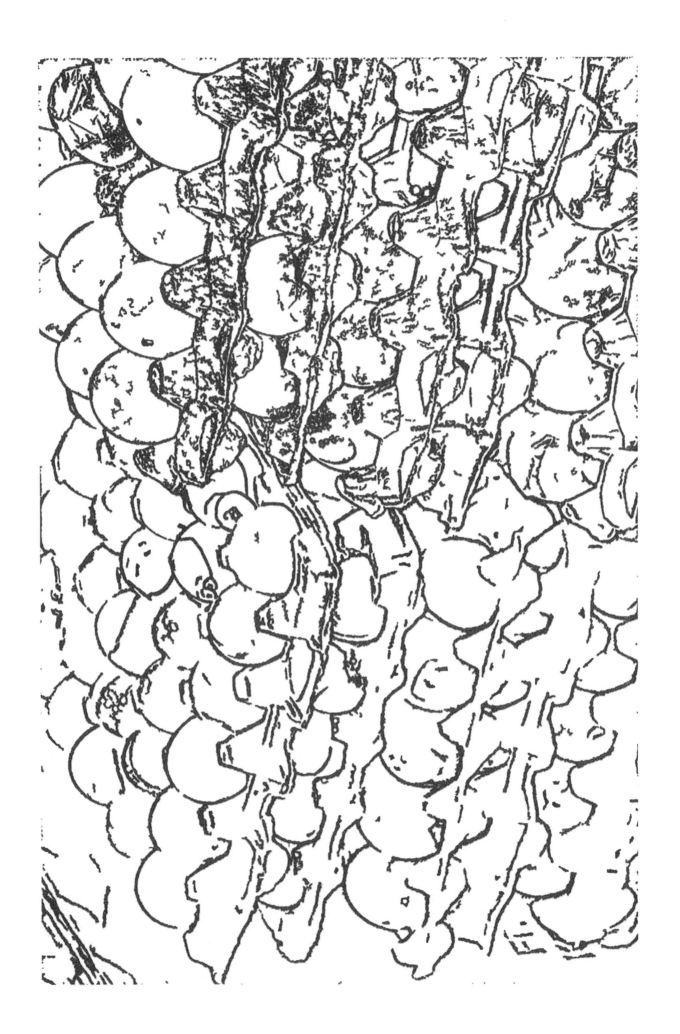

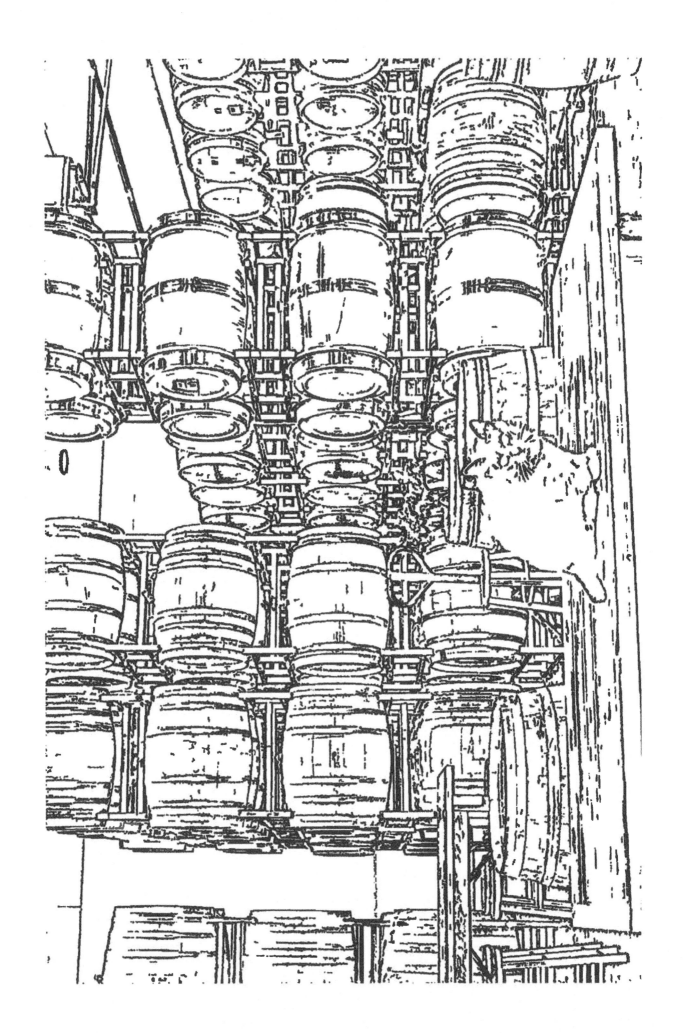

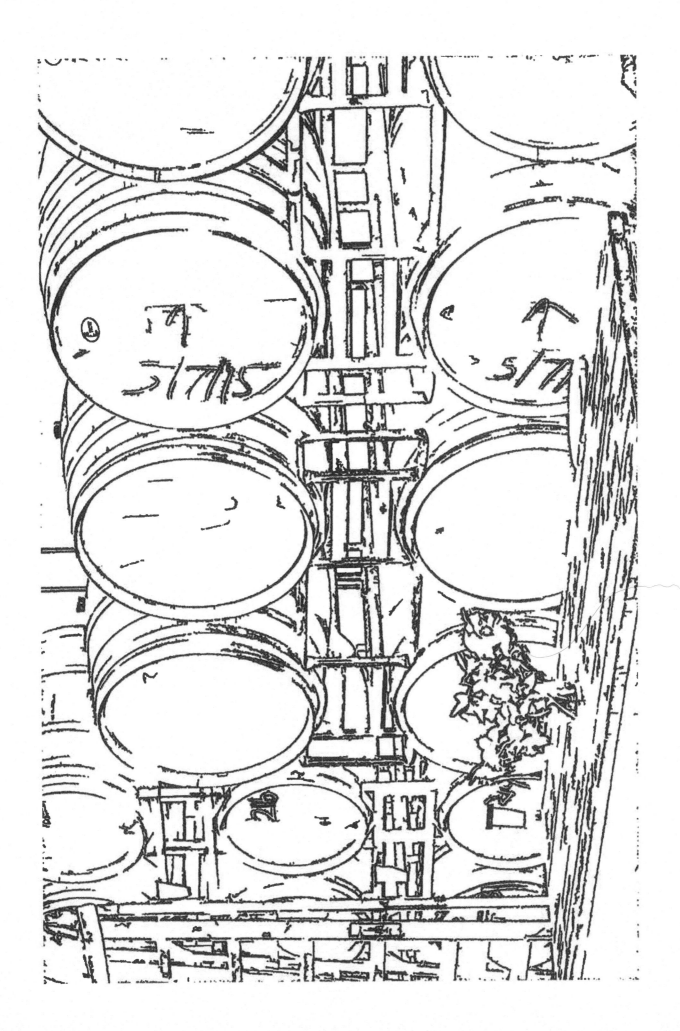

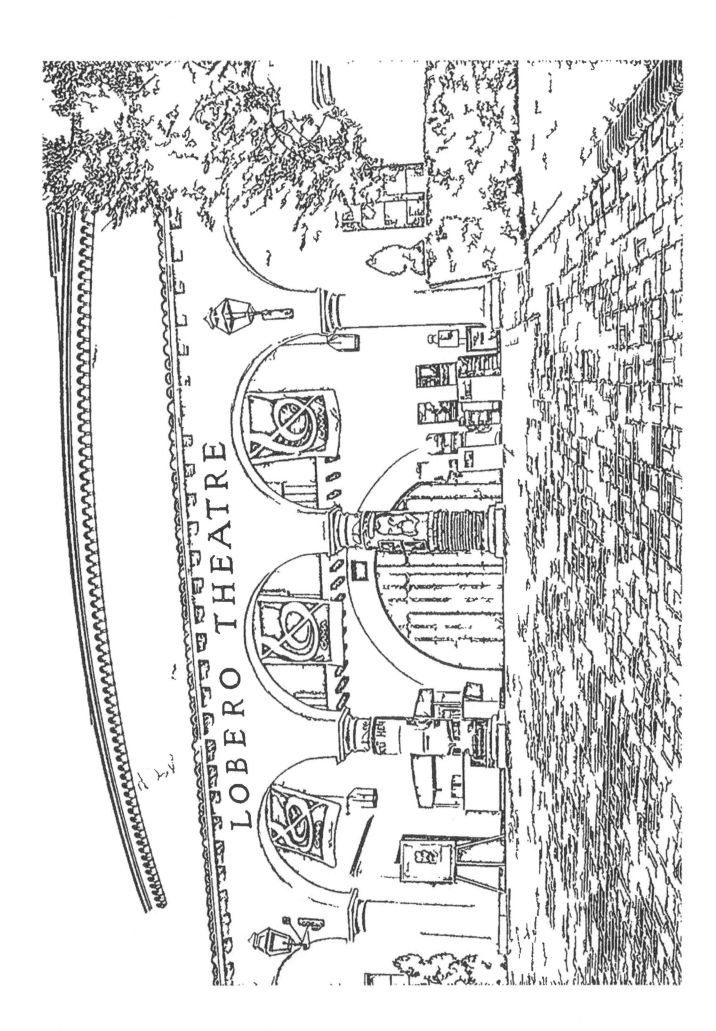

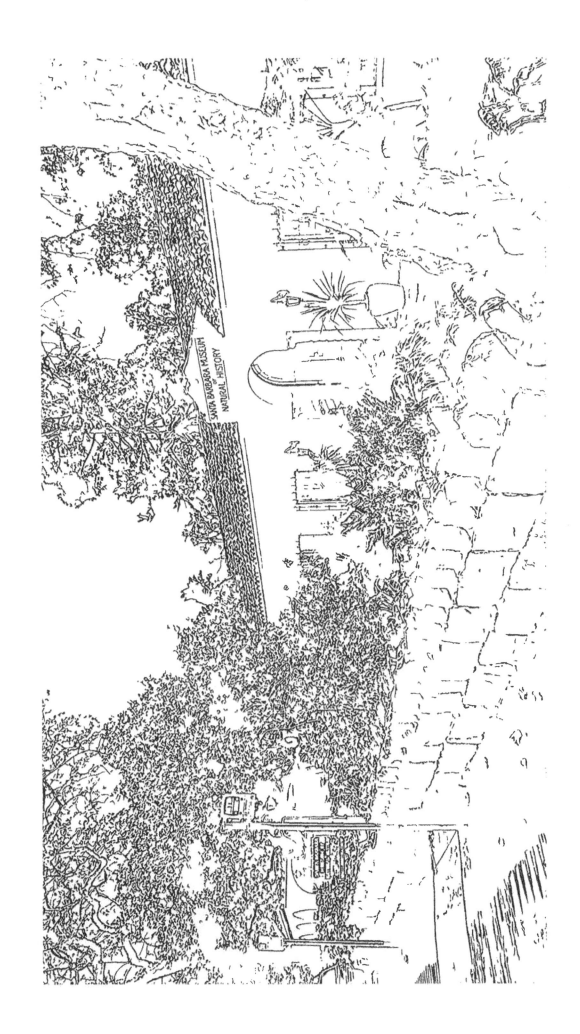

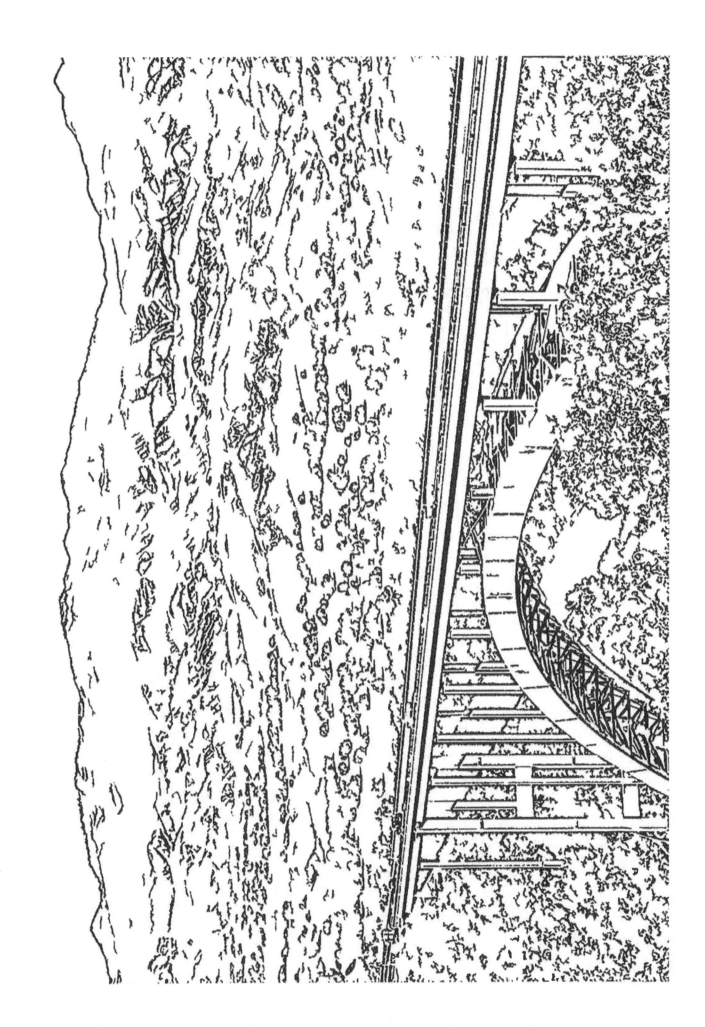

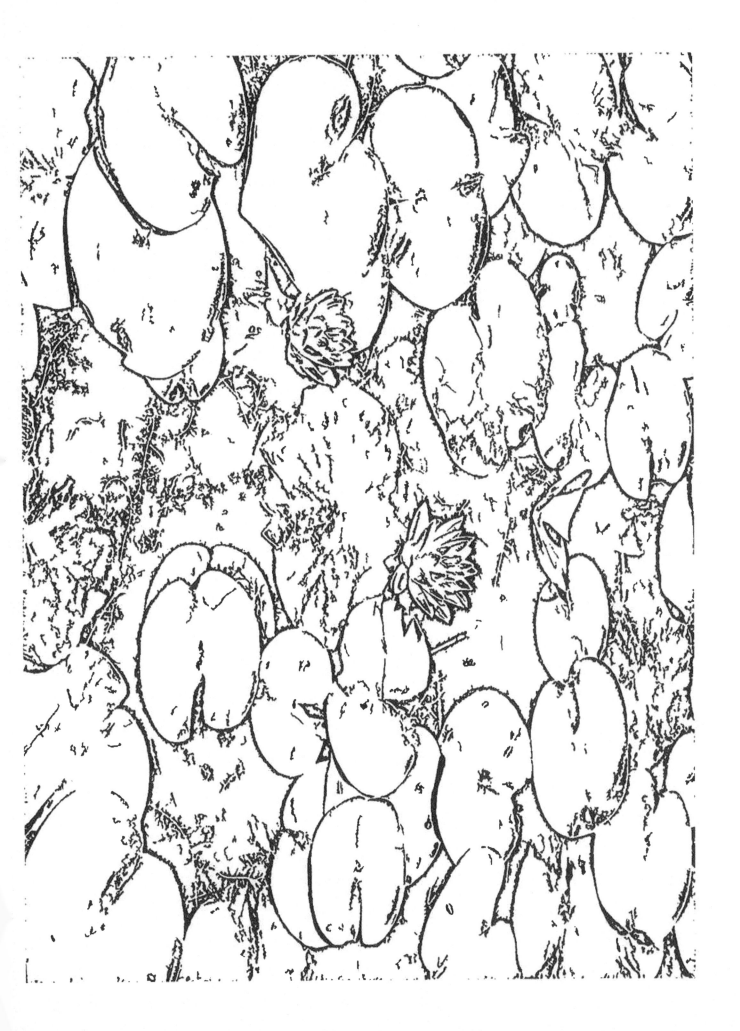

Made in the USA
Las Vegas, NV
08 January 2023

65272911R00031